Water Bullet!

by Dawn Bluemel Oldfield

Consultant: Jenny Montague
Assistant Curator of Marine Mammals
New England Aquarium
Boston, Massachusetts

BEARPORT
PUBLISHING

NEW YORK, NEW YORK

Credits

Cover, © Tyson Mackay/All Canada Photos/SuperStock; TOC, © Christian Musat/Shutterstock; 4–5, © Tyson Mackay/All Canada Photos/SuperStock; 6, © Ingrid Visser/Hedgehog House/Minden Pictures; 7, © Ingrid Visser/SeaPics; 8L, © Howard Hall/SeaPics; 8TR, © Mark Conlin/SeaPics; 8BR, © Chris Newbert/Minden Pictures; 9, © John Hyde/AlaskaStock; 10T, © Gerard Lacz/Peter Arnold, Inc./Alamy; 10B, © Juniors Bildarchiv/Alamy; 11, © Hiroya Minakuchi/Minden Pictures; 12, © Flip Nicklin/Minden Pictures; 13, © Francois Gohier/Ardea; 14, © Charles Hood/Oceans Image/Photoshot; 15, © Rolf Hicker/All Canada Photos/SuperStock; 16, © Amos Nachoum/SeaPics; 17, © Marty Snyderman/Corbis/SuperStock; 18, © Suzi Eszterhas/Minden Pictures; 19, © Brandon D. Cole/Brandon Cole Marine Photography; 20–21, © Tyson Mackay/All Canada Photos/Getty Images; 22, © Martin Ruegner/Photolibrary; 23TL, © Marty Snyderman/Corbis/SuperStock; 23TR, © Condor 36/Shutterstock; 23BL, © Suzi Eszterhas/Minden Pictures; 23BC, © Francois Gohier/Ardea; 23BR, © Steve Estvanik/Shutterstock.

Publisher: Kenn Goin
Editorial Director: Adam Siegel
Creative Director: Spencer Brinker
Design: Debrah Kaiser
Photo Researcher: Picture Perfect Professionals, LLC

Library of Congress Cataloging-in-Publication Data

Bluemel Oldfield, Dawn.
  Killer whale : water bullet! / by Dawn Bluemel Oldfield ; consultant, Jenny Montague.
    p. cm. — (Blink of an eye: Superfast animals)
  Includes bibliographical references and index.
  ISBN-13: 978-1-936087-92-1 (library binding)
  ISBN-10: 1-936087-92-8 (library binding)
  1. Killer whale—Juvenile literature. I. Title.
  QL737.C432B59 2011
  599.53'6—dc22
                                    2010015003

For more information, write to Bearport Publishing Company, Inc., 101 Fifth Avenue, Suite 6R, New York, New York 10003. Printed in the United States of America in North Mankato, Minnesota.

072010
042110CGE

10 9 8 7 6 5 4 3 2 1

Contents

A Speedy Swimmer

The killer whale is one of the fastest animals in the sea.

It can move through the water at a speed of up to 30 miles per hour (48 kph).

That's six times faster than a swimmer in an Olympic race.

The world's fastest human can swim at a top speed of about 5 miles per hour (8 kph). A great white shark can swim at a top speed of 25 miles per hour (40 kph). A killer whale can swim faster than both.

Human
5 mph / 8 kph

Great White Shark
25 mph / 40 kph

Killer Whale
30 mph / 48 kph

A World of Whales

Killer whales live in every ocean in the world.

They may live in shallow waters close to **shore** or in deeper waters farther out.

Killer Whales in the Wild

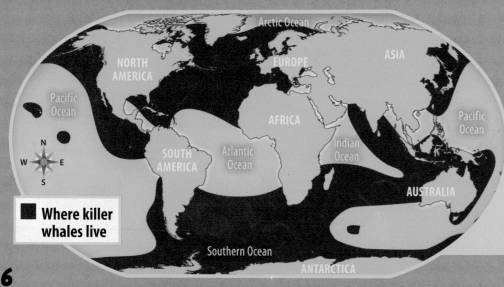

Where killer whales live

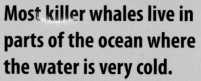

Most killer whales live in parts of the ocean where the water is very cold.

Because killer whales are such fast swimmers, in one day they can travel up to 100 miles (161 km).

Sea Food

Killer whales find food in their ocean homes.

Some killer whales feast mainly on squid and on fish, such as salmon.

Others feed mostly on sea lions and seals.

Sometimes killer whales even eat other kinds of whales, such as gray whales.

salmon

gray whale

sea lion

A killer whale can be up to 32 feet (10 m) long and weigh about 22,000 pounds (9,979 kg). These big animals need to eat a lot—up to 500 pounds (227 kg) of food each day.

Water Bullet

A killer whale shoots through the water to catch its **prey**.

Its bullet-shaped body is covered with smooth skin, so water passes over it easily.

The whale's large tail moves up and down, pushing the animal forward.

A triangle-shaped fin on its back helps keep it from rolling over as it speeds ahead.

back fin

tail

back fin

tail

Killer whales have to be fast because the animals they hunt move quickly, too. A sea lion, for example, can swim up to 25 miles per hour (40 kph).

Surprise Attacks

A killer whale doesn't catch prey only in water.

That's because sea lions spend part of their time on land.

To look for them, a killer whale pokes its head out of the water.

Once the whale spots its prey, it swims toward it with lightning speed.

It launches itself onto the beach and grabs its victim in its strong jaws.

Then the whale catches a wave to carry it back into the sea.

Killer whales have up to 56 cone-shaped teeth that are up to five inches (13 cm) long. The shape of their teeth helps them rip and tear into prey.

killer whale attacking a sea lion

Deep Dives

Sea lions dive into the water to swim and hunt.

When they do, killer whales are quick to follow them.

The whales can dive down at least 600 feet (183 m) to catch these animals.

That's 36 times deeper than an Olympic diving pool.

Killer whales are **mammals**. They cannot breathe underwater. Instead, they must come up to the surface for air. Luckily, a killer whale can hold its breath and stay underwater for as long as 27 minutes.

A Deadly Disguise

Speed and strength are a killer whale's main weapons.

Its colors, however, also help it hunt.

They act as **camouflage**.

The black back of a killer whale blends in with the ocean's dark, deep water.

Animals that are swimming above the whale often can't see it—until it's too late.

black back

Sea creatures swimming under a killer whale can also get caught by surprise. The whale's white belly blends in with the light, sunlit surface of the water.

white belly

Terrific Teamwork

Killer whales live in families called **pods**.

Often, the members of a pod use teamwork to catch their food.

Sometimes they surround a large group of fish so they can't swim away.

Other times they surround another whale.

They take turns biting and ramming it until the victim is weak and injured.

Then the killer whales share their meal with one another.

pod

A pod may be made up of only 3 killer whales or as many as 40.

19

Safe Waters for Whales

Because killer whales are so fast and powerful, other sea animals don't hunt them.

However, the whales are still often in danger.

Humans sometimes dump trash and chemicals into the ocean, which can make the animals sick.

Luckily, people are working to make the oceans cleaner.

By doing so, the waters will become safer for these swift and skillful swimmers.

The United States and some other countries have laws that protect killer whales from being hunted, captured, or harmed.

Built for Speed

What makes a killer whale such a fast swimmer? Here is how different parts of the animal's body help it reach its amazing speeds.

large fin on its back keeps it from rolling over as it swims

body is bullet-shaped, which lets water pass over it easily—and not slow the whale down as it moves forward

flippers at sides help with steering

long, powerful tail moves up and down to push the whale through the water

camouflage (KAM-uh-flahzh) colors and markings on an animal's body that help it blend in with its surroundings

mammals (MAM-uhlz) animals that are warm-blooded, nurse their young with milk, and have hair or fur on their skin at some point in their lives

pods (PODZ) family groups of whales

prey (PRAY) animals that are hunted and eaten by other animals

shore (SHOR) the land along the edge of a lake, river, or ocean

23

Index

Read More

Arnold, Caroline. *A Killer Whale's World.* Mankato, MN: Picture Window Books (2006).

Lunis, Natalie. *Killer Whale: The World's Largest Dolphin.* New York: Bearport (2010).

Simon, Seymour. *Killer Whales.* New York: SeaStar Books (2002).

Learn More Online

To learn more about killer whales, visit
www.bearportpublishing.com/BlinkofanEye

About the Author

Dawn Bluemel Oldfield is a freelance writer who lives in Prosper, Texas, just north of Dallas.